Gone to Sanctuary

From the Sins of Confusion

GONE TO SANCTUARY
FROM THE SINS OF CONFUSION

PHOTOGRAPHS BY

JOHN S. KIEWIT

CAPRA PRESS
SANTA BARBARA

Cover photo: Moscow, Idaho

Cover design, book design and typography
by Frank Goad, Santa Barbara

Printed by Palace Press International in China

First Edition, limited printing of 1,000 casebound, 3,000 softbound

Library of Congress Cataloging-in-Publication Data
Kiewit, John S., 1948-
Gone to Sanctuary : from the sins of confusion / photographs by John S.
Kiewit. — 1st ed.
p. cm.
ISBN 0-88496-422-1 (hardcover : alk. paper) - ISBN 0-88496-423-X (pbk. : alk. paper)

1. Landscape photography--West (U.S.) 2. Photography, Artistic. 3. West (U.S.)--
Pictorial works. 4. Kiewit, John S., 1948-   .
Title.
TR660.5.K54   1997
779'.3678--dc21   97-3464 CIP

CAPRA PRESS
POST OFFICE BOX 2068
SANTA BARBARA, CALIFORNIA

For Linda Linnick Kiewit
who was with me all the way.

PREFACE

I HAVE SPENT A GOOD PART OF THE PAST THIRTY YEARS planning a trip or traveling to geography off the tourist itinerary. In the Western States I became familiar with places obscure and remote, and in the process came to know myself and the landscape as I found it.

The highways and trails leading to sometimes never-reached destinations have offered up solitude and grandeur, apprehension and beauty, knowledge and grief. Along the route and at road's end, the decay of man's dreams and the simple elegance of the natural scene have been the premier attractions. The pattern of dunes, the color of sheet metal, the weathering of wood and the changing sky are images that are as important to me as the 'grand view'. The pleasure in finding and photographing these subjects has never wavered, but has become more alluring over the years—the joy of the finding.

In addition to my own journals, my partners in the search have been books; authors whose words became part of the photographs that I was looking to make.

Many nights, cocooned in a camper, I reread paragraphs and thought how those remarks pertained to certain images. In this text I have used some of my own remembrances together with words by favorite writers to frame my photographs.

I have destroyed my boots trying to dry them over campfires; eaten weird concoctions of my own making; imbibed with strangers; run out of gas; broken down; gotten lost; fallen into icy streams; been stuck in the mud, sand and snow; had major sunburn and blisters; started and ended love; been sick as a dog; and have made friends with some real odd people.

I am no sooner home than I feel the pull to be off again. I suppose it's a type of sickness. Doubtful recovery.

—JOHN S. KIEWIT

INTRODUCTION

IN TRYING TO DESCRIBE THE AMERICAN WEST, Gertrude Stein said, "Conceive a space filled with moving." John Kiewit's landscapes show just that: a vast empire where animals and human beings have lived and laid claim. His eye makes our eye move all over the place. The images are meandering, lonely, wild, forgiving, and bring us to those places that give us sanity and solace. We are happy in each temporary abode, among trees, stacked mountain ranges, swimming through curdled clouds and oceans of grass.

John is native to the California coast. We met when I came to live on this ranch just under the bent elbow of Point Conception. I was sick when I moved into my unheated cabin; he brought a pickup load of wood and his home-made chicken soup. We had both come here seeking sanctuary from confusion.

John's photographs result from a lifetime of roaming through the western states. In Nevada we see the burnt-out shell of an abandoned De Soto far from any town, the exterior of a bar with a drive-up window in Coolridge, New Mexico, a fence in Utah wandering across coral pink dunes, an orange railroad car converted into a house with turquoise doors in Nogales, Arizona, and closer to home, a lighthouse keeper's lonely house protected by the curved arm of a tree. But there is unity to these peregrinations. As John Steinbeck said, "This journey has been like a full dinner with many courses." An appropriate quote. John Steinbeck would have loved John Kiewit's cooking as well as his acerbic wit.

John roams, but is at home everywhere. That is his gift. He sees into the heart of a place and gives us images that make us want to go there, move on, and come back again. His path is circular. He isn't giving us freak shows. Rather, these photographs are the ones we would make of the places we've loved if we were able. John has done it for us and I thank him.

—GRETEL EHRLICH
Agua Caliente Canyon
December 5, 1996

"There was no where to go but everywhere, keep rolling under the stars, the western stars."

—JACK KEROUAC

"Follow the double yellow line of wheel tracks through the sand and rock and you will find a habitation somewhere huddled in a protected place, with a few trees pointing their roots at the under-earth water, a patch of starveling corn and squash, and strips of jerky hanging on a string. There is a breed of desert men, not hiding exactly but gone to sanctuary from the sins of confusion."

—John Steinbeck

BENTON, NEVADA

"If we are always arriving and departing, it is also true that we are eternally anchored. One's destination is never a place but rather a new way of looking at things."

—HENRY MILLER

DEATH VALLEY, CALIFORNIA

"Rare is the American who has not dreamed of dropping whatever he is doing and hitting the road. The dream of unrestrained movement is a distinctly American one. An inheritance bequeathed to subsequent generations by those restless souls who populated the American continent. Travel—away from here, toward a vague distant destination—is part of our national folklore."

—DAVID NICHOLS

Los Alamos, California

Arriving late always makes me crazy. In some instances I wasn't even born yet.

*—*J*OURNAL* E*NTRY*, *November 1982*

RIDGEWAY, COLORADO

"I am usually very calm over the displays of nature, but you will scarce believe how my heart leaped at this. It was like meeting one's wife. I had come home again."

—ROBERT LOUIS STEVENSON

DIXIE FOREST, UTAH

"A countryman has a place on earth that is his own, and much as he may love to wander, as I myself do, he loves the wandering more because he has a place to return to, a place where he belongs."

—EDWARD ABBEY

ELGIN, OREGON

"There was a house made of dawn. It was made of pollen and of rain, and the land was very old and everlasting. There were many colors on the hills, and the plain was bright with different-colored clays and sands. Red and blue and spotted horses grazed in the plain, and there was a dark wilderness on the mountains beyond. The land was still and strong. It was beautiful all around."

—N. Scott Momaday

OWENS LAKE, CALIFORNIA

"All America lies at the end of the wilderness road, and our past is not a dead past, but still lives in us. Our forefathers had civilization inside themselves, the wild outside. We live in the civilization they created, but within us the wilderness still lingers. What they dreamed, we live, and what they lived, we dream."

—T. K. WHIPPLE

BODIE, CALIFORNIA

"I love all waste
And solitary places;
where we taste the pleasure of believing
what we see
Is boundless, as we wish
our souls to be"

—P. B. SHELLEY

SIERRA, CALIFORNIA

"When we presently got underway…, I became a new being, and the subject of my own admiration. I was a traveler! A word had never tasted so good in my mouth before. I had an exultant sense of being bound for mysterious lands and distant climes which I never have felt in so uplifting a degree since. I was in such a glorified condition that all ignoble feelings departed out of me, and I was able to look down and pity the untraveled with a compassion that had hardly a trace of contempt in it."

—MARK TWAIN

TOMALES, CALIFORNIA

"It is good to have an end to journey towards; but it is the journey that matters in the end."

—Ursula K. Le Guin

CERRO GORDO ROAD, CALIFORNIA

The old mining towns of central Nevada were both exhilarating and troubling. The population and structures seem tied by an invisible thread to the last century. The photographic possibilities were numerous; yet, it was as if a pall hung over the region leaving me wishing I was elsewhere.

—JOURNAL ENTRY, November 1979

AUSTIN, NEVADA

"…old buildings, old people on a front porch…strange how old, obsolete buildings and plants and mills, the technology of fifty or a hundred years ago, always seems to look so much better than the new stuff…Nature has a non-Euclidian geometry of her own that seems to soften the deliberate objectivity of these buildings with a kind of random spontaneity that architects would do well to study."

—ROBERT M. PIRSIG

MODENA, UTAH

"The mighty West looms vast before my sight,
bright in the mystery of sun and sky;
mesa and plain, the desert and the sown,
the scar-faced mountains and the blinding snows,
the deathless blue and soaring angel-clouds;
and on its farthest rim I see my soul
arise, broad-winged and free, and beckon me."

—MAYNARD DIXON

FUNERAL RANGE, CALIFORNIA

"I have written much about many places. But the best places of all, I have never mentioned."

—EDWARD ABBEY

"The noise of the wilderness is varied; it has no monotony; it is the music of the earth of which man is an integral part whether he knows it or not."

—WILLIAM O. DOUGLAS

McGee Creek, California

"Though we travel the world over to find the beautiful, we must carry it with us or we find it not."

—Ralph Waldo Emerson

SAN MIGUEL, CALIFORNIA

I had some trouble getting my old VW camper up to Elkhorn. At that elevation, the carburetor wasn't getting enough oxygen and my lurching speed dwindled to about 3 m.p.h. with intermittent stalling. Able to go no further, I blocked the tires with rocks and walked a quarter mile up to what had been Main Street. It was like a picture postcard lost for nine decades in the mail.

—JOURNAL ENTRY, *April 1969*

ELKHORN, MONTANA

"Never has man produced a more lonely sound than the whistle of a steam locomotive. It was a sad sound that seemed to say to each of us who heard it: 'Come with me and I'll show you America…'"

—Hood River Blackie

VALLE, ARIZONA

"Man always kills the thing he loves, and so we the pioneers have killed our wilderness. Some say we had to. Be that as it may, I am glad I shall never be young without wild country to be young in. Of what avail are forty freedoms without a blank spot on the map?"

—Aldo Leopold

LOS ALAMOS, CALIFORNIA

Did I ever see an old, wood building I didn't like? Maybe, but not often. The ghosts tell of work, hope, success, and defeat; stories always worth listening to.

—JOURNAL ENTRY, May 1995

KEOUGH HOT SPRINGS, CALIFORNIA

"Go as far as you dare in the heart of a lonely land, you can not go so far that life and death are not before you."

—MARY AUSTIN

ALABAMA HILLS, CALIFORNIA

"In the West the past is very close. In many places, it still believes it's the present."

—JOHN MASTERS

WILLAMINA, OREGON

Motoring up to old Taos with Woody Guthrie singing how he had followed his footsteps "to the sparkling sands of diamond deserts," we were told upon arrival that the Pueblo was closed. While reflecting that we had never heard of an entire community being shut, Woody continued his lament that "this land was made for you and me."

—JOURNAL ENTRY, *December 1977*

TAOS PUEBLO, NEW MEXICO

"There is a stage in every quest, every journey, when you seem hopelessly suspended between where you were and where you are bound. There is a beauty to such journeys that knocks logic to smithereens."

—ROB SCHULTHEIS

RANCHOS DE TAOS, NEW MEXICO

"Roam abroad in the world, and take thy fill of its enjoyments before the day shall come when thou must quit it for good."

—Sa' Di Gulistan

BERLIN, NEVADA

63

I had been out photographing the empty Carrizo Plain. Heading home I came across 'Wild Bill' who had just hand-painted his Kaiser automobile and was about to start on the house.

—JOURNAL ENTRY, *December 1991*

POZO, CALIFORNIA

"The living of life, any life, involves great and private pain, much of which we share with no one. In such places as the Inner Gorge the pain trails away from us. It is not so quiet there or so removed that you can hear yourself think, that you would even wish to; that comes later. You can hear your heart beat. That comes first."

—BARRY LOPEZ

CANYON DE CHELLY, ARIZONA

"A thousand hills lay bare to the sky, and half was fallow ground; and all of them, with the shallow valleys between, seemed big and strange and isolated. The beauty of them was austere, as if the hand of man had been held back from making green his home site…"

—ZANE GREY

CAMP ROBERTS, CALIFORNIA

"All journeys in the desert are pilgrimages. You come out wiser, with some of the cheap shine worn off."

—Rob Schultheis

HANKSVILLE, UTAH

71

"Journeys, like artists, are born and not made. A thousand differing circumstances contribute to them, few of them willed or determined by the will—whatever we may think. They flower spontaneously out of the demands of our natures—and the best of them lead us not only outwards in space, but inwards as well. Travel can be one of the most rewarding forms of introspection…"

—LAWRENCE DURRELL

BIG SUR, CALIFORNIA

"I have seen almost more beauty than I can bear."

—Everett Ruess

YOSEMITE VALLEY, CALIFORNIA

"Only by going alone in silence, without baggage, can one truly get into the heart of the wilderness. All other travel is mere dust and hotels and baggage and chatter."

—John Muir

CALF CREEK, UTAH

The best spring water I ever tasted, coupled with the coldest nights, made trips to the high desert memorable. Strange characters in lonely places added to the mix.

—JOURNAL ENTRY, *December 1976*

BODIE, CALIFORNIA

"But our trip was different. It was a classic affirmation of everything right and true and decent in the national character. It was a gross, physical salute to the fantastic possibilities of life in this country—but only for those with true grit. And we were chock full of that."

—HUNTER S. THOMPSON

GONZALES, CALIFORNIA

"The emptiness of the West was for others a geography of possibility."

—GRETEL EHRLICH

KANAB, UTAH

"The statement 'To travel is better than to arrive' comes back to mind again and stays. We have been traveling and now arrive. For me a period of depression comes on when I reach a temporary goal like this and have to reorient myself toward another one."

—Robert M. Pirsig

POINT REYES, CALIFORNIA

I was waiting around for the sun, drinking harsh coffee and listening to Mozart. It was one of those windy mornings that make your bones ache and your nose run. As the light brought in the color, I stopped bitching about almost everything.

—JOURNAL ENTRY, *January 1993*

PIGEON POINT, CALIFORNIA

"Traveling is *seeing*; it is the implicit that we travel by."

—Cynthia Ozick

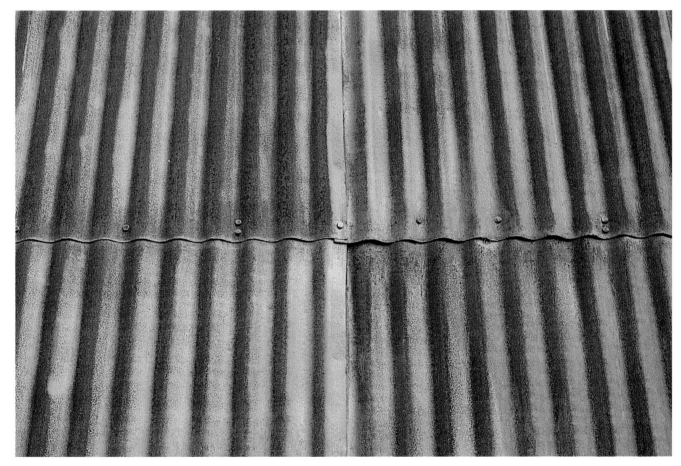

COOS BAY, OREGON

"You cannot travel on the path
Before you have become the path
Itself"

—Buddha

GLORIETA, NEW MEXICO

91

"It was a hard country, nothing nice or comfortable about it. It was only gorgeous."

—ROB SCHULTHEIS

PANAMINT RANGE, CALIFORNIA

"…as in a dream we zoomed through small crossroad towns smack out of darkness, and passed long lines of lounging harvest hands and cowboys in the night. They watched us pass in one motion of the head, and we saw them slap their thighs from the continuing dark on the other side of town—we were a funny looking crew."

—JACK KEROUAC

CASTROVILLE, CALIFORNIA

"Mind you, it is mostly men who go into the desert, who love it past all reasonableness, slack their ambitions, cast off old usages, neglect their families because of the pulse and beat of a life laid bare to its thews and sinews. Their women hate with implicitness the life like the land, stretching interminably whitey-brown, dim and shadowy blue hills that hem it, glimmering pale blue waters of mirage that creep and crawl about its edges."

—Mary Austin

GABBS, NEVADA

The bar patrons of Silver City were an odd lot. Some were refugee hippies from San Francisco, others had come down from the mountains to a place where, in the words of one, "There ain't no high-rise trees!" Outsiders were made to feel less than welcome.

—JOURNAL ENTRY, November 1971

SILVER CITY, NEVADA

"We are kept on the move by continual reminders of the lateness of the hour…nature signals to us in her numerous ways that we'd best get our ass in gear while we can, because the summer is never going to last, my darlings, never. Just now a flock of geese passing over calls out to me 'Go South! Follow the sun! If you wait too long it will be too late.' And I get all manicky just hearing them…"

—KEN KESEY

SONORA, CALIFORNIA

"On countless nights when I lay half-sleeping in my grandmother's house I heard the midnight train go by. We were so close, in that narrow village, that it was right under my window…How musical that whistle, how fantastic that passage of tumult and lights, what romance and joy went by on the midnight train!"

—R. L. DUFFUS

CALIENTE, NEVADA

"We would like to live as we once lived but history will not permit it."

—John F. Kennedy

"Let us probe the silent places
Let us seek what luck betide us."

—Robert W. Service

GOODING, IDAHO

My wife Linda and I rented a houseboat on Lake Powell in a vain attempt to find the remains of Glen Canyon. Looking into the depths, I could only imagine what others had been privileged to see.

—JOURNAL ENTRY, January 1978

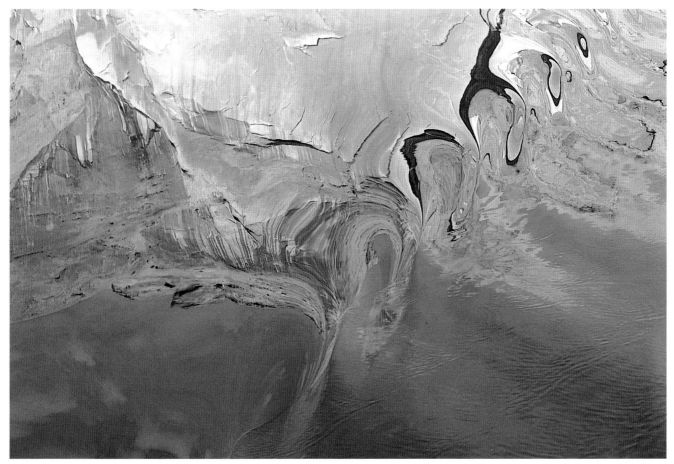

LAKE POWELL, UTAH

"The bare uncompromising face of the land is too much for us to behold, and so we clothe it in myth, sentiment, and imposed expectations."

—Robert Finch

CHACO CANYON, NEW MEXICO

"Time is like a river made up of the events that happen, and its current is strong; no sooner does anything appear than it is swept away, and another comes in its place, and will be swept away too."

—MARCUS AURELIUS

PUEBLO BONITO, NEW MEXICO

The 'Big Empty' is how I think of that area which borders on Oregon, Nevada, and Idaho. Traveling there, it's almost a shock when a cluster of buildings and people pop up out of the void.

—JOURNAL ENTRY, *April 1978*

JORDAN VALLEY, OREGON

"Time is a flowing river. Happy those who allow themselves to be carried, unresisting, with the current. They float through easy days. They live, unquestioning, in the moment."

—CHRISTOPHER MORLEY

MERCED RIVER, CALIFORNIA

"A person's purpose is nothing more than to rediscover through detours of art, or love, or passionate work, those one or two images in the presence of which his heart first opened."

—Albert Camus

LOWELL, OREGON

The watchman had been giving me a lot of visual insubordination and finally walked over to ask why I was photographing the abandoned building. "I think it's beautiful," I said. "It was better with people," he mused.

—JOURNAL ENTRY, *June 1992*

SANTA MARIA, CALIFORNIA

"The beaten track is often the best track, but devote your time to the by-ways. In no other way can you so quickly reach the heart of the country."

—FRANK TATCHELL

KING CITY, CALIFORNIA

123

"…though he was coming from as far as progress had reached, he belonged to an older time."

—WENDELL BERRY

HIGHWAY 41, NEW MEXICO

"I have been a stranger in a strange land."

—THE BIBLE

SAUSALITO, CALIFORNIA

We had partied on into the night with a group of climbers from Camp Four. I thought I could freshen up the next morning by jumping into the icy Merced River; which was only the first mistake I made that day.

—Journal Entry, February 1968

YOSEMITE VALLEY, CALIFORNIA

"We simply need that wild country available to us, even if we never do more than drive to its edge and look in. For it can be a means of reassuring ourselves of our sanity as creatures, a part of the geography of hope."

—WALLACE STEGNER

GARRAPATA, CALIFORNIA

"Never mind. The mountains are calling…"

—JOHN MUIR

SIERRA RANGE, CALIFORNIA

"God gives all men all earth to love but, since man's heart is small, ordains for each one spot shall prove beloved over all."

—RUDYARD KIPLING

BIG SUR, CALIFORNIA

"So the West drew to itself more than its share of unsettlers, of people whose essential relation to place was the denial of place. And yet places that they came to, being the last place to go, finally took hold of them, drew them down into their flinty soils, rooted them, claimed them, shaped them the way they shaped sagebrush."

—Daniel Kemmis

BASALT, COLORADO

"I like to take the car as far as I can go up a two-track, then get out and walk until the road disappears. This is the only solution to the neurotic pang that you might be missing something."

—JIM HARRISON

CAPITOL REEF, UTAH

Familiar as I am to saloons, beer halls and bars, the drive-up window conjured up visions I hadn't touched on before.

—*JOURNAL ENTRY, April 1979*

COOLRIDGE, NEW MEXICO

"We asked a passenger who belonged there what sort of a place it was. 'Well,' said he, after considering, and with the air of one who wishes to take time and be accurate, 'It's a hell of a place.' A description which was photographic for exactness."

—MARK TWAIN

BELLINGHAM, WASHINGTON

143

"I suspect the road is a young man's chore and that time is the most relentless highway of all, but I know that old ribbon of asphalt ain't quite through with me yet."

—JAMES CRUMLEY

HIGHWAY 395, CALIFORNIA

"Walk on a rainbow trail,
Walk on a trail of a song,
And all about you will be beauty."

—Navajo Song

MINARETS WILDERNESS, CALIFORNIA

"Those who contemplate the beauty of the earth find reserves of strength that will endure as long as life lasts."

—RACHEL CARSON

BENTON, CALIFORNIA

In those days, West Marin County was still oyster and dairy country. At the post office & store in Marshall you could get your mail, a beer and some gas. Old Bruce, who ran the place, had an original Marilyn Monroe calendar on the wall just above the dusty cans of beans and spam.

—JOURNAL ENTRY, May 1973

MARSHALL, CALIFORNIA

"You have to get over the color green; you have to quit associating beauty with gardens and lawns; you have to get used to an inhuman scale."

—WALLACE STEGNER

LEES FERRY, ARIZONA

"Every part of this country is sacred to my people. Every hillside, every valley, every plain and grove has been hallowed by some fond memory or some sad experience of my tribe. The soil is rich with the life of our kindred."

—Chief Seattle

SANTA ROSA ISLAND, CALIFORNIA

"There's a race of men that don't fit in.
A race that can't stand still;
So they break the hearts of kith and kin
And roam the world at will."

—ROBERT WILLIAM SERVICE

POINT CONCEPTION, CALIFORNIA

"You sea! I resign myself to you also—I guess what you mean,
I behold from the beach your crooked inviting fingers,
I believe you refuse to go back without feeling of me,
We must have a turn together, I undress,
Hurry me out of sight of land,
Cushion me soft, rock me in Billowy Drowse.
Dash me with amorous wet, I can repay you."

—WALT WHITMAN

CENTRAL COAST, CALIFORNIA

I had been living in Carmel, feeling pretty insignificant photographically. One December a series of great storms rolled through exposing the beach rock and washing away the menial debris of summer.

—JOURNAL ENTRY, *February 1983*

CARMEL, CALIFORNIA

"For always roaming with a hungry heart, much have I seen and known."

—ALFRED TENNYSON

HILTON CREEK, CALIFORNIA

"...I wondered what it must be like to be born in a place like this, where only the foreground—the porch, the store-front, the main street—mattered."

—Paul Theroux

VIRGINIA CITY, NEVADA

"Only the air spirits know
What lies beyond the hills,
Yet I urge my team farther on
Drive on and on
On and on"

—ESKIMO POEM

ZUNI, NEW MEXICO

"This journey had been like a full dinner of many courses, set before a starving man. At first he tries to eat all of everything, but as the meal progresses he finds he must forgo some things to keep his appetite and taste buds functioning."

—John Steinbeck

CUYAMA, CALIFORNIA

The road to Ouray had begun to wear on me. I wanted to be there, have a bath, and hopefully get a good meal. There have been times when I felt an obligation to the camera.

—JOURNAL ENTRY, *May 1987*

HIGHWAY 145, COLORADO

"A place belongs forever to whoever claims it hardest, remembers it most obsessively, wrenches it from itself, shapes it, renders it, loves it so radically that he remakes it in his image."

—JOAN DIDION

SALINAS, CALIFORNIA

"It's a shame to take this country away from the rattlesnakes."

—D. W. GRIFFITH

SANTA BARBARA COUNTY, CALIFORNIA

"A place has almost the shyness of a person, with strangers; and its secret is not to be surprised by too direct interrogation."

—ARTHUR SYMONS

PLEASANT HILL, OREGON

The house had been built by Italian immigrants for the family who kept the lighthouse functioning. It was joyful to think of storms it had survived and the people who had lived there. Leaving such a place, despite its isolation, must have been sad.

—JOURNAL ENTRY, December 1988

BIXBY RANCH, CALIFORNIA

"The Pacific is my home ocean; I knew it first, grew up on its shore, collected marine animals along the coast. I know its moods, its color, its nature. It was very far inland that I caught the first smell of the Pacific. When one has been long at sea, the smell of land reaches far out to greet one. And the same is true when one has been long inland."

—JOHN STEINBECK

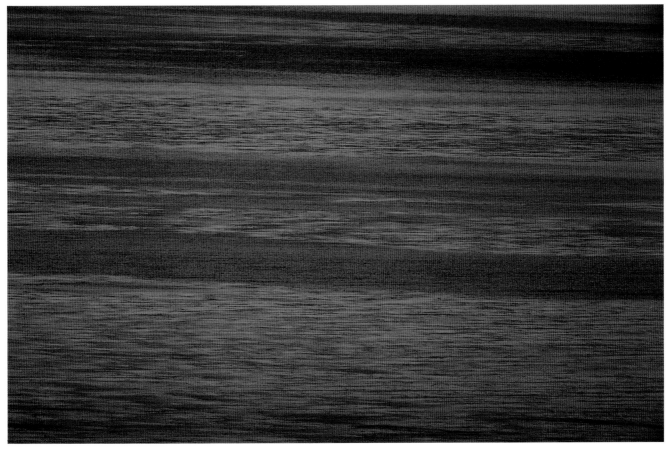

CARMEL, CALIFORNIA

"We use the word 'wilderness' but perhaps we mean wildness. Isn't that why I've come here? In wilderness, I seek the wildness in myself—and in so doing, come on the wildness everywhere around me because, after all, being part of nature, I'm cut from the same cloth."

—Gretel Ehrlich

McGee Canyon, California

"There are places and moments in which one is so completely alone that one sees the world entire."

—Jules Renard

EUREKA VALLEY, CALIFORNIA

Listening hard to the strange sound coming from my VW bus as I traveled across Nevada, I turned left onto Hwy. 395 at Mono Lake and began to parallel the east side of the Sierra. Arriving at 'Tom's Place' for gas and a beer, I walked around a bit really pleased to be away from the internal combustion engine.

—Journal Entry, *May 1985*

Tom's Place, California

"The journey is the reward."

—TAO SAYING

MARBLE CANYON, ARIZONA

"One always begins to forgive a place as soon as it's left behind."

—Charles Dickens

SILVER CITY, IDAHO

"Often, when following the trail which meanders over the hills, I pull myself up in an effort to encompass the glory and the grandeur which envelops the whole horizon. Often, when the clouds pile up in the north and the sea is churned with white caps, I say to myself: 'This is the California that men dreamed of years ago, this is the Pacific that Balboa looked out on from the Peak of Darien, this is the face of the earth as the Creator intended it to look.'"

—HENRY MILLER

POINT SAL, CALIFORNIA

"The treasure which you think not worth taking trouble and pains to find, this one alone is the real treasure you are longing for all your life. The glittering treasure you are hunting for day and night lies buried on the other side of that hill yonder."

—B. Traven

CEDAR BREAKS, UTAH

"O public road, I say back I am not afraid to leave you,
        yet I love you,
You express me better than I can express myself."

—WALT WHITMAN

REHOBOTH, NEW MEXICO

197

My friend Jamie hunted through our cooler while I set up the camera. "Why did we stop here?" she asked. I was too ecstatic to answer.

—JOURNAL ENTRY, *March 1996*

NECANICUM, OREGON

"The true mystery of the world is the visible, not the invisible."

—Oscar Wilde

JACOB LAKE, ARIZONA

La Favorita looked like it had been my kind of place. Ballads, yarns, history and maybe some local legends had been born inside those doors. It's a shame to see a neighborhood shrine fall into decay.

—JOURNAL ENTRY, *November 1986*

"Watching the circling seasons, listening to the songs of the waters and winds and birds, would be an endless pleasure. And what glorious cloud-lands I would see, storms and calms, a new heaven and a new earth every day."

—JOHN MUIR

POINT CONCEPTION, CALIFORNIA

205

"Each precious moment entails every other. Each sacred place suggests the imminent presence of all places."

—EDWARD ABBEY

CHANNEL ISLANDS, CALIFORNIA

"What is a ruin but time easing itself of endurance."

—Djuna Barnes

VOLCANO, CALIFORNIA

The trip to Convict Lake had been uneventful. When I finally arrived I discovered fishing season had kicked in. Just as I was leaving the masses for a more solitary experience, I noticed something I had previously passed by a dozen times.

—JOURNAL ENTRY, May 1993

CONVICT LAKE, CALIFORNIA

"…Bits of East and Middle West are buried here and there in the West, but none of the true West is buried in the East."

—WALLACE STEGNER

GAVIOTA, CALIFORNIA

"The trees and their lovers will sing their praises, and generations yet unborn will rise up and call them blessed."

—JOHN MUIR

YOSEMITE VALLEY, CALIFORNIA

"The finest workers in stone are not copper or steel tools, but the gentle touches of air and water working at their leisure with a liberal allowance of time."

—HENRY DAVID THOREAU

ALEGRIA CANYON, CALIFORNIA

"The difference between landscape and landscape is small, but there is a great difference between the beholders."

—Ralph Waldo Emerson

DILLON, CALIFORNA

Heading up to Grover Hot Springs I hoped I would arrive before serious weather. Although it was clear, the radio was telling of a gathering storm. I passed up one good campsite after another, reminding myself of past episodes.

—JOURNAL ENTRY, *April 1994*

EBBETTS PASS, CALIFORNIA

"There's something about the desert that doesn't like man, something that mocks his nesting instinct and makes his constructions look feeble and temporary. Yet it's just that inhospitableness that endears the arid rockiness, the places pointy and poisonous, to men looking for its discipline."

—William Least Heat Moon

RHYOLITE, NEVADA

"The late dreary wilderness brightened into a fine open country, with stately groves, and clumps of oaks of a gigantic size, some of which stood singly, as if planted for ornament and shade, in the midst of rich meadows; while our horses, scattered about, and grazing under them, gave to the whole the air of a noble park."

—Washington Irving

PASO ROBLES, CALIFORNIA

"An hour before daylight the wind came up and swept along the floor of the desert, moving the sand, changing the shapes of the hummocks under the dark mesquite. It blew across the bare mesas, over the summit stones of the mountains, down to a desert river flowing south through a pass where hills pitched steep to the edges of the narrowed water. Below the pass, the wind followed the stream into a valley where it found the houses of a lonely town sleeping by trees and plowed fields."

—Tom Lea

BROWNS VALLEY, CALIFORNIA

"One place is everywhere
Everywhere is nowhere"

—Persian Proverb

NOGALES, ARIZONA

229

We had been bushwhacking through low scrub, tick country when we were stopped by an irate property owner who demanded to know if we were 'tree huggers.' A question that didn't really pertain to our geographic locale.

—*Journal Entry, August 1985*

SANTA YNEZ, CALIFORNIA

"There is a third dimension to traveling, the longing for what is beyond."

—Jan Myrdal

MALIBU, CALIFORNIA

I grew up in Malibu before it was a big deal. The old pier, now closed, served a fisherman's breakfast for $1.25 that would last most of the day. I wasn't much of an angler, but I loved that old cafe.

—*JOURNAL ENTRY, December 1972*

MALIBU, CALIFORNIA

"Certain places seem to exist mainly because someone has written about them."

—JOAN DIDION

ANTELOPE VALLEY, CALFORNIA

"I frequently tramped eight or ten miles through the deepest snow to keep an appointment with a beech tree, or a yellow birch, or an old acquaintance among the pines."

—HENRY DAVID THOREAU

PACIFIC GROVE, CALIFORNIA

Hiking over 10,600' Kearsarge Pass was an interesting venture. The trail was deserted and the scenery spectacular. At Bull Frog Lakes we met a roving Park Ranger who informed us that dogs and campfires were prohibited; two rules that were soon violated without much remorse.

—JOURNAL ENTRY, September 1981

KINGS RIVER REGION, CALIFORNIA

"I like little towns with their handfuls of buildings huddled close to the grain elevators, like medieval towns clustered around their cathedrals."

—Gordon Webber

PETALUMA, CALIFORNIA

"One of the gravest problems when traveling away from our dream coasts is getting a cup of coffee in which you can't see a dime on the bottom."

—JIM HARRISON

CHAMA, NEW MEXICO

"Probably no one alive hasn't at one time or another brooded over the possibility of going back to an earlier, ideal age in his existence and living a different kind of life. It is perhaps mankind's favorite daydream."

—Hal Boyle

ELK MEADOWS, UTAH

Walking through my current hometown, I realized that it is not always necessary to travel a great distance, lug cameras, backpacks, etc. in order to find an appealing image.

—JOURNAL ENTRY, *November 1995*

SANTA BARBARA, CALIFORNIA

"For my part, I travel not to go anywhere, but to go. I travel for travel's sake. The great affair is to move."

—ROBERT LOUIS STEVENSON

DRAKES POINT, CALIFORNIA

"Backward amid the twilight glow
Some lingering spots yet brightly show
          On hard roads won;
Where still some grand peaks mark the way
Touched by the light of parting day
          And memory's sun."

—John C. Fremont

ACKNOWLEDGMENTS

Page 11: From ON THE ROAD by Jack Kerouac. Copyright © 1955, 1957 by Jack Kerouac; renewed © 1985 by Stella Kerouac and Jan Kerouac. Used by permission of Viking Penguin, a division of Penguin Books USA Inc.

Page 12: From TRAVELS WITH CHARLEY by John Steinbeck. Copyright © 1961, 1962 by The Curtis Publishing Co., © 1962 by John Steinbeck, renewed © 1990 by Elaine Steinbeck, Thom Steinbeck, and John Steinbeck IV. Used by permission of Viking Penguin, a division of Penguin Books USA Inc.

Page 14: From BIG SUR AND THE ORANGES OF HIERONYMOUS BOSCH by Henry Miller. Copyright © 1957 by New Directions Publishing Corp. Reprinted by permission of New Directions Publishing Corp.

Page 16: From INTRODUCTION TO ERNIE'S AMERICA by David Nichols. Copyright © 1989 by Random House, Inc.

Page. 20: From ACROSS THE PLAINS by Robert Louis Stevenson.

Page 22: From DOWN THE RIVER by Edward Abbey. Copyright © 1982 by Edward Abbey. Used by permission of Dutton Signet, a division of Penguin Books USA Inc.

Page 24: From HOUSE MADE OF DAWN by N. Scott Momaday. Copyright © 1966, 1968 by N. Scott Momaday. Used by permission of HarperCollins Publishers Inc.

Page 26: From STUDY OUT THE LAND by T. K. Whipple. Copyright © 1985. Ayer Company Publishers.

Page 28: From JULIAN AND MADDALO by Percy Bysshe Shelley.

Page 30: From LIFE ON THE MISSISSIPPI by Mark Twain. Copyright © 1874. Houghton & Company.

Page 32: From THE LEFT HAND OF DARKNESS by Ursula K. Le Guin. Copyright © 1985. Warner Publishing, Inc.

Page 36: From ZEN AND THE ART OF MOTORCYCLE MAINTENANCE by Robert M. Pirsig. Copyright © 1974 by Robert M. Pirsig. Used by permission of William Morrow & Company, Inc.

Page 38: From "Home-Land" by Maynard Dixon in RIM ROCK AND SAGE: THE COLLECTED POEMS OF MAYNARD DIXON (with drawings; Introduction by Kevin Starr). Copyright © 1977 by California Historical Society, San Francisco. Used by permission of the California Historical Society, San Francisco.

Page 40: From A VOICE CRYING IN THE WILDERNESS by Edward Abbey. Copyright © 1989 by Edward Abbey. Used by permission of St. Martin's Press.

Page 42: From A WILDERNESS BILL OF RIGHTS by William O. Douglas. Copyright © 1965 by William O. Douglas. Used by permission of Little, Brown and Company Publishers.

Page 44: From ESSAYS by Ralph Waldo Emerson.

Page. 48: From 'Home on the Rails: A Veteran Hobo Turns Historian in Recalling his Favourite Characters from the Heyday of Rail-Riding,' by Hood River Blackie. *Quest Magazine,* August/September, 1978.

Page 50: From A SAND COUNTY ALMANAC by Aldo Leopold. Copyright © 1966 by Aldo Leopold. Used by permission of Oxford University Press, Inc.

Page 54: From THE LAND OF LITTLE RAIN by Mary Austin. Copyright © 1903 by Mary Austin. Used by permission of University of New Mexico Press.

Page. 56: From PILGRIM SON by John Masters.Copyright © 1971 by John Masters. Used by permission of William Morris Agency, Inc.

Page 60: From THE HIDDEN WEST by Rob Schultheis. Copyright © 1982 by Rob Schultheis. Used by permission of Random House, Inc.

Page 62: Sa' Di Gulistan 1258.

Page 66: From CROSSING OPEN GROUND by Barry Lopez. Copyright © 1989 by Barry Lopez. Used by permission of Sterling Lord Literistic.

Page 68: From THE DESERT OF WHEAT by Zane Grey. Copyright © 1919 by Zane Grey. Used by permission of Zane Grey Inc.

Page 70: From THE HIDDEN WEST by Rob Schultheis.

Page 72: From BITTER LEMONS by Lawrence Durrell. Copyright © 1957 by Lawrence Durrell. Used by permission of Curtis Brown, Ltd., London on behalf of The Estate of Lawrence Durrell.

Page 74: From A VAGABOND FOR BEAUTY by Everett Ruess. Copyright © 1983 by Gibbs M. Smith, Inc.

Page 76: From THE YOSEMITE by John Muir. Copyright © 1912. Reprint, Garden City, N.Y.: Doubleday and Company and The Natural History Library, 1962.

Page 80: From FEAR AND LOATHING IN LAS VEGAS by Hunter S. Thompson. Copyright © 1971 by Hunter S. Thompson. Used by permission of Random House, Inc.

Page 82: From THE SOLACE OF OPEN SPACES by Gretel Ehrlich. Copyright © 1985 by Gretel Ehrlich. Used by permission of Viking Penguin, a division of Penguin Books USA Inc.

Page 84: From ZEN AND THE ART OF MOTORCYCLE MAINTENANCE by Robert M. Pirsig.

Page 88: From ENCHANTERS AT FIRST ENCOUNTER by Cynthia Ozick. Copyright © by Cynthia Ozick. Used by permission of Random House, Inc.

Page 92: From THE HIDDEN WEST by Rob Schultheis.

Page 94: From ON THE ROAD by Jack Kerouac.

Page 96: From "The Land" in STORIES OF THE COUNTRY OF LOST BORDERS by Mary Austin. Copyright © 1903 by Mary Austin. Used by permission of University of Nevada Press.

Page 100: From SOMETIMES A GREAT NOTION by Ken Kesey. Copyright © 1964, renewed 1992 by Ken Kesey. Used by permission of Viking Penguin, a division of Penguin Books USA Inc.

Page 102: From THE MIDNIGHT TRAIN by R. L. Duffus. Copyright © 1930. Longmans Green & Company.

Page 104: From Speech at Fort Worth, Texas, November, 1963 by John F. Kennedy.

Page 106: From "Call of the Wild" in THE SPELL OF THE YUKON by Robert W. Service.

Page 110: From "Into the Maza" in THE PRIMAL PLACE by Robert Finch. Copyright © 1983 by Robert Finch. Used by permission of W.W. Norton & Company.

Page 112: Marcus Aurelius, Roman Emperor, 121-180 A.D.